BIRDS OF A FEATHER

POEMS BY
JANE YOLEN

PHOTOGRAPHS BY
JASON STEMPLE

FOREWORD BY
DONALD KROODSMA, PH.D.

WORDSONG

Honesdale, Pennsylvania

To *the memory of our first bird watcher,*
David Stemple, and to the next two
generations of birders in the family

—J.Y.

For *my father—if it's about birds,*
he deserves all the credit.

—J.S.

Birds of a feather flock together,
And so will pigs and swine;
Rats and mice will have their choice,
And so will I have mine.

—*Mother Goose*

The publisher thanks Dr. John H. Rappole, an ornithologist
and the chairman of the board of trustees of the Roger Tory
Peterson Institute, and Dr. Donald Kroodsma, professor
emeritus of biology at the University of Massachusetts,
Amherst, and a Fellow of the American Ornithologists'
Union, for reviewing the text and photographs.

Wordsong
An Imprint of Boyds Mills Press, Inc.
815 Church Street
Honesdale, Pennsylvania 18431
Printed in the United States of America

ISBN: 978-1-59078-830-1
Library of Congress Control Number: 2010929592

First edition
The text of this book is set in 14-point Sabon.

10 9 8 7 6 5 4 3 2 1

Front cover: *least bittern (Ixobrychus exilis);*
back cover: American oystercatchers
   (Haematopus palliatus);
page 1: brown pelicans (Pelecanus occidentalis)
   in nonbreeding plumage;
page 2: black-necked stilt (Himantopus
   mexicanus);
page 4: painted bunting (Passerina ciris).

CONTENTS

Foreword

As an ornithologist and obsessed with the details in the daily lives of birds, I know these eagles and chickadees and kingfishers and the other fine birds in this book. But after absorbing the poems and photographs here, I'll never see these birds again in the same way. The kingfisher no longer has a crest but a "blue Mohawk"; the chickadee is not "black-capped" but instead has a "black cap on." The highly aggressive kingbird is a "flying ninja"; the predatory great horned owl "the night's dark harrower." And the hooded merganser will forever carry a marshmallow in its head!

Scientists collect numbers and study the details, but these poems and photographs give us another angle, reminding us that birds are far more than an accumulation of facts. If "God touched the bird— and so, it flies" (my favorite line in the book), Jane Yolen and Jason Stemple are themselves God's helpers. The birds in this book are not confined to the pages here but, instead, soar into our lives.

—Donald Kroodsma, Ph.D.

The Regal Eagle

The regal eagle sits alone
upon a tree that serves as throne.
But sometimes when the eagle flies
(though this might come as some surprise)
a mob of crows may—wing to wing—
together drive away that king.
Democracy in beak and claw
finds regal eagle's fatal flaw.
And is that legal? I don't know.
You'll have to ask a mobster crow.

A *mature bald eagle* (Haliaeetus leucocephalus) *is ten times heavier than a crow and has a wingspan that is more than twice its size. But when crows get together, they have been known to attack an eagle, going for the head from above and behind, staying well clear of its beak and talons. Eagles are birds of prey, and though they are mainly fish eaters, they occasionally eat small birds and mammals. So crows will sometimes mount preemptive strikes on an eagle, dive-bombing the larger bird even though it may be far away from any nests. This attack behavior is called mobbing.*

Chickadee-dee

Plump little fellow
With your black cap on.
Sweet little puffball
With your black cap on.
Call out your cheery *chick-a-dee-dee*.
I will leave some seeds for you-free-free.
You can hide them all from me-me-me
With your black cap on.

The black-capped chickadee (Poecile atricapillus) is a hoarder, hiding seeds and other food to eat at a later time. Everything goes into a different storage place. Amazingly, days and weeks later, the chickadee can find thousands of hidden goodies. The "chick-a-dee-dee" is considered by birdsong specialists to be a "call." But when a chickadee whistles "fee-bee-ee," experts say that is the bird's actual "song."

Haiku for a Cool Kingfisher

Hey, girl, fish lover,
Sitting on the dead gray tree,
Love the blue Mohawk.

Belted kingfishers (Megaceryle alcyon) dive into the water after small fish. Also on the menu: crayfish and frogs and sometimes insects. A kingfisher kills or stuns larger fish by holding the fish in its beak and thwacking the prey against a tree branch or perch.

The wood duck (Aix sponsa) *can be found in wooded swamps and in streams, ponds, and lakes. One of the few North American ducks that nest in tree holes, the wood duck also uses man-made nesting boxes. The day after wood ducklings hatch, they jump to the ground and often waddle many yards away to find a body of water, because they already know how to swim.*

A Solitary Wood Duck

In the green scene,
in the emerald setting,
where pondweed chokes
the green, green waters,
one thing is not green.
A solitary wood duck—
    face glowing,
    flag face showing
    its colors,
    like an admiral's warship—
sails unconcernedly through all that green.
    We surrender,
    we surrender,
    we surrender to your beauty.

Whooo Is the Great Horned Owl?

Who hears mice cowering in the field, under dry grass,
in tunnels, runnels, burrows, beneath dirt?
Who makes rabbits hop away in fright, scream at night?
Who is silent-winged, feather-fringed, air-muted, ear-tufted?
Who claims the name of night's dark harrower?
Whoo-whoo whoooooo whoo-whoo?
I doo-doo doooooo doo.

The great horned owl (Bubo virginianus) *has "ear tufts"
made of feathers, though these are not actual ears. The
owl's real ears are small holes located on either side of its
head. The ear tufts convey the owl's moods. When the bird
is irritated or angry, the ear tufts lie flat; when the bird is
curious, those ear tufts stand straight up.*

The royal tern (Thalasseus maximus), *larger than most other kinds of terns, is a member of the gull family. Royal terns nest in dense, packed colonies, usually by the ocean.*

Terns Galore

At the seaside, terns galore,
One tern, one tern, one tern more.
I tern. You tern.
My turn to fly, tern,
Overhead and high, tern.
Underneath and 'bye, tern.
Why, tern, *why* turn?
Turning terns are all returning,
There upon the shore.

Northern Mockingbird:
A Threesome Haiku

I speak as you speak,
Sing as you sing, or better.
I am your echo.

I am not a clone,
But can be mistaken for
The original.

Three times I sing you.
Before I find a new song,
I mock you three times.

The northern mockingbird (Mimus polyglottos), like all "mockers," is known for its ability to mimic other birds' songs. A mocker repeats at least three passages of a song before going on to a different bird's tune. A mockingbird often sings up to nine echoes of another bird's song.

19

American oystercatchers (Haematopus palliatus) *are part of a group of birds called waders. They can be found strolling about in fields and estuaries—as well as on seashores and boardwalks, making what is described as a continuous kleep or bleep sound.*

Oystercatchers on Parade

Like a bunch of windup toys,
Oystercatchers on parade,
Unafraid,
Strutting out with a kleeping noise.
Who notices the brown wings, the shock of that black head?
Who notices the pink legs, spotlight eyes?
Instead,
All we see is orange bill, orange bill, orange bill,
A signal lamp, a traffic cone,
A poster for a chemical spill,
While oystercatchers, unafraid,
Continue on their stiff parade,
Like little windup children's toys
Marching on with a kleeping noise.

Eastern Kingbird: The Flying Ninja

Such an unassuming bird,
you look like a shadow,
a modest minister
in gray and black and brown.
But I know your secret:
you are a spy, a guerilla,
a ninja of the air,
and any who get close to your nest
better take care.
Better take care.

*Nest predators and larger birds better be wary
of eastern kingbirds (Tyrannus tyrannus). They
regularly attack hawks and crows that venture too
near kingbird nests.*

The hooded merganser (Lophodytes cucullatus) *is a small, strange-looking diving* *duck. Its long and slender bill has a hooked nail at the end, which is perfect for* *catching fish, frogs, mud crabs, crayfish, clams, aquatic insects, and insect larvae.* *Like wood ducklings, hooded merganser babies leave their hole-in-a-tree nest and* *head for water within twenty-four hours of their hatching.*

Questions to Ask a Hooded Merganser

Is that a marshmallow in your head?
Are those Navy stripes on your shoulder?
Are you wearing a big white bib?
Do you like the water warmer? Colder?

Can you use your beak like a pencil?
Does some barber trim your down?
Is there a reason your face makeup
Makes you look like a circus clown?

Please answer in under ten words—that's best.
I have to get it right on the test.

Cedar Waxwings
Unmasked

Who are these masked birds?
Not Robin Hoods,
for they live in
the open woods.
They only deal
in stolen goods
like berry futures,
cedar cones,
and sweet, sweet fruit
(but leave the stones).
Insects they catch
on the fly
when swarms of them
go buzzing by.
No need to worry,
moan, or fret.
Your valuables
they will

        not

          get.

Cedar waxwings (Bombycilla cedrorum), *with their rakish black masks, gather in large flocks to eat insects in the spring and berries and other fruit in the fall. They do not live in the deep woods, like Robin Hood, but in the more open woodlands and nearby farms and orchards.*

27

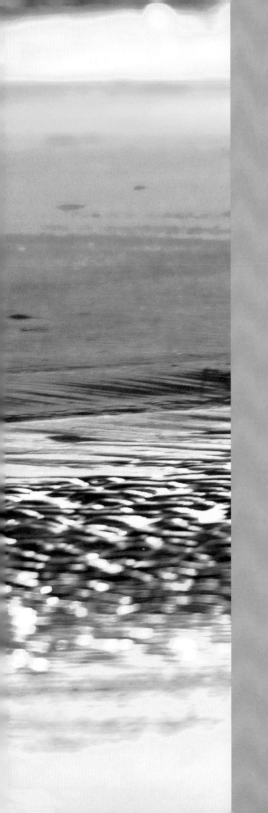

Sandpipers' Haiku

Three sandpipers run
Across a sunrise shingle
Signaling the dawn.

Sandpiper *is the common name for a number of different wading birds in the Scolopacidae family. They use their long, slender beaks as tools to probe into the sand to find food.*

29

Rufous-Sided Towhee

Well named, little bird,
With your rufous siding,
As if the painter had run out
Of ordinary brown,
Mixing what little was left
With a bit of orange
To brighten your day—and mine.

The rufous-sided towhee was thought to be a single species until the early 2000s. Experts now believe there are two distinct species. The one on this page, a female, is called the eastern towhee (Pipilo erythrophthalmus), and the other is a western bird called the spotted towhee (Pipilo maculatus). They each have different songs as well as regional dialects. However, the female towhees do not sing. That's for the males to do.

The marbled godwit (Limosa fedoa) is a long-beaked, long-legged shorebird. One of several kinds of godwits, it uses that strange bill to probe in the sand or mud for food such as clams, crabs, snails, bristle worms, and leeches.

Creation of the Marbled Godwit

I wonder if God's helper on that fifth day—
making all the birds of the air—
was so new to the business of creation,
he approached it with little care.

Clearly he'd small grasp of structure;
his understanding of form—absurd.
Only a fumbling, bumbling fool
could have designed this Godwit bird.

Its beak belongs to a larger creature;
its head is really too small;
its back and belly do not match
the rest of it at all.

And yet, much to the maker's surprise,
God touched the bird—and so, it flies.